How societies perceive murder

Victoria Liberman

Contests

Introduction

Murder is generally defined as the unlawful killing of a person with malice afterthought. In other words, it needs two things: *actus reus* (an unlawful action) and *mens rea* (knowing that the action is unlawful and going ahead with it nonetheless). There can be no question that murder is the crime that is given most attention by the media and by society in general (D'Cruze *et al.* 2006: 23). The reason for this is not hard to see: the violent and premature end to someone's life deeply disturbs the human psyche, partly because it reminds us that we are mortal and that the same thing could happen to us. Of course the media plays an enormous role in making a big deal out of murders, but the truth is that it takes two to tango: the media has a vested interest in presenting news in such a way as to sell as many copies as possible or achieve high ratings on TV, but on the other hand overemphasising murders would not be a part of this if it did not tap into society's fascination with the subject.

In this dissertation it will be argued that murder is simply an extreme form of crime – of course it is particularly traumatic and its effect is permanent, but nevertheless it is ultimately just a crime and not special in any way beyond the considerable damage it does. The issue here is of course that society tends to think of murderers as an aberration, pathological, and exceptionally evil – whichever term is used to describe murderers, the point is that society likes to think of them as 'not us' (D'Cruze et *al.* 2006: 23). This phenomenon is made even stronger by the language that judges and prosecutors like to use in the United Kingdom: it is very common for judges to use the word 'evil' when sentencing people who have been found guilty of murder – this is what D'Cruze et *al.* referred to as 'Gothic rhetoric' (D'Cruze et *al.* 2006: 157). In this dissertation it will be attempted to show that although murder is correlated with a number of socio-economic factors, the truth is that a huge variety of people have committed murder and the correct conclusion to draw from this is that they are not fundamentally different to those who have never murdered – they were simply subject to the circumstances (past and present) that led them to commit murder. I am excluding of course the minority of murderers who were genuinely mentally ill and for whom the 'them and us' distinction is a little more understandable.

Chapter I

Sociological theories of crime

Criminology generally aims to find the causes for criminal behaviour. Although it is true that criminology has spent very little effort on explaining murder, a discussion of some of the sociological theories of crime is nevertheless useful because it shows that murder (and other crimes) is correlated with an enormous amount of variables, which means that almost no one is immune to it.

1.1 The anomie hypothesis

The anomie hypothesis was first proposed by Durkheim, and was later refined by Merton (Adler & Laufer 1995) who developed it and adapted it to be United States. The theory of anomie basically proposes that criminal behaviour is stimulated by the fact that society leads individuals to have very high expectations and hopes in their lives, but then fails to give equal opportunities to everyone, with the result that many people become disillusioned and bitter. This conflict between high expectations and practical disappointment leads some people to abandon society's norms and achieve their goals without paying attention to the laws. Merton describes this as 'social structural strain' (Vold et *al.* 2002: 135). Of course the importance of anomie is very obvious in crimes such as theft and fraud but it is also relevant to murder – as Lukes (1967, cited in Rock 2002) wrote: 'this condition [anomie] would lead a man to commit suicide and homicide'. So, since any human being can be the victim of anomie, it follows that any human being can also end up committing murder.

One implication of this theory is that if society emphasizes the result (wealth and success) more than the process (living and law-abiding life) this will increase crime rate, including murder. This is what happens in the United States. The 'strain' that Merton refers to tends to affect the lower classes much more than anyone else (Vold et *al.* 2002: 137). The theory was criticized by Kornhauser (1978), on the grounds that expectations in delinquents were pretty low, which must mean that there was no strain. However, she used the wrong variables in investigating this: she asked delinquents about their aspirations regarding education and proper jobs and found that their aspirations in this field very low. This is not surprising, because the whole point of delinquents is that they no longer believe education and honest employment are the way forward. Research done later by Bernard (1984) asked delinquents about their aspirations relating to money, enjoyment and women – he found that their aspirations in this field are very high and that they resort to crime, including murder, to satisfy them.

One piece of evidence that supports the anomie theory is the observation that the United States have the highest homicide rate in the world (FBI, 2004). This matches the fact that the 'American dream' produces very high hopes and expectations in the population in the United States, which means that disappointment is particularly bad when individuals realise that society probably will not let them achieve their ambitions (or only with difficulty). In the United States there is also a very big difference between what the state wants (laws) and what individuals in many cultural groups want (Vold et al. 2002: 138). This makes anomie worse because it gives them a very strong sense that they will never catch up with the wealthy and powerful if they have obey laws and do as they are told.

The theory of anomie, also known as strain theory, includes two separate mechanisms: structural and cultural. The cultural idea is that certain subcultures are simply more willing to break the law, perhaps because they feel disadvantaged and abandoned by the government. The structural idea is that although in the United States the 'American dream' affects everyone in all classes, the real opportunities to make that dream come true are much more common in the upper classes than in the lower classes. So although most people in the United States experience anomie, people in the lower classes experience it particularly badly and are therefore more likely to choose a life of crime, because opportunities are not symmetrically distributed. This probably explains why all types of crime, including murder, are much more common in the lower classes than in the upper classes. This observation has been confirmed by many studies, including the work done by Kim & Pridemore (2005), who found that poverty and socio-economic instability is positively correlated with homicide in Russia.

1.2 The Chicago School

The term 'Chicago School' refers to the research done by social ecologists at the University of Chicago in the 1920's. Social ecology is the study of the abundance and distribution of humans. Their main argument was that as cities grow they naturally develop distinct zones that house different social classes: the central zone (business district) is surrounded by a ring known as the transition zone, which tends to be inhabited by immigrants, ethnic minorities and other poor and disadvantaged people. This zone is surrounded by very stable working class housing which in turn is surrounded by comfortable middle-class housing. A transition zone is much more likely to be affected by problems such as mental illness, poverty and of course crime – in other words the 'transition zone is co-extensive with social pathology' (Rock 2002: 61). This idea makes sense, because being unable to spend time with people from other social classes makes it more likely that collective resentment and criminal tendencies will develop. This brings us on to Sutherland's Differential Association Theory (Sutherland, 1947) which is essentially part of the Chicago school of thought.

1.3 Differential Association Theory

Sutherland's theory basically states that people pick up criminal tendencies and desires from other people (professional criminals). It is clear how this relates to the more general Chicago School: people are more likely to engage in criminal behaviour and become professional criminals if they spend time with criminals, because the message from the crime world will be stronger than the message from law-abiding society. An important part of Sutherland's theory is that the learning process happens in intimate social groups. Intimate social groups with criminal tendencies are more likely to form if the zonation of cities is also in place – as Sutherland put it: 'in some societies an individual is surrounded by persons who invariably define the legal codes as rules to be observed, while in others he is surrounded by persons whose definitions are favourable to the violation of the legal codes' and 'a person becomes delinquent because of an excess of definitions favourable to the violation of law over definitions unfavorable to the violation of the law. This is the principle of *Differential Association*' (Sutherland 1947: 6-7).

Sutherland's theory was so important and influential that it attracted quite a lot of criticism. One major criticism that can be made is that the correlation between the company kept by criminals and the fact that they are criminals does not imply that one caused the other. In other words, although the association is definitely observable it does not mean that spending time in the company of professional criminals will turn a law-abiding citizen into a criminal. On the other hand, it is undoubtedly true that people with criminal tendencies tend to associate and spend time together, which is natural and easy to understand: 'birds of a feather flock together.' Sutherland argued that spending time in the company of professional criminals was more likely to cause criminal behaviour in the observer if the frequency, duration and intensity of these encounters was sufficient (Sutherland, 1947).

Another criticism was that Sutherland's theory of Differential Association is not testable in a scientific way. To be tested scientifically we would have to prove that the number of definitions that favour the law was greater than the number of definitions that favour crime before the person became a criminal, and that the opposite was true when the person became a criminal (Glueck, 1956).

The theory proposed by Wolfagang & Ferracuti (1981) is especially relevant to this essay because they dealt specifically with criminal violence. They argued that there is a 'subculture of violence' among the lower classes that makes violent behaviour much more likely, even if the circumstances are trivial. My argument in this essay is that murder should be seen as nothing more than an extreme crime which does not require mental illness or other special circumstances, and this is supported by Wolfgang and Ferracuti's description of crimes of passion, which involved very normal people who were almost never mentally ill or special in any other way. The importance of mental illness in the murder is overemphasised by the media, which likes to present murderers as 'monsters'. The truth is of course that even if a correlation is found between mental illness and murder it does not necessarily mean that the mental illness caused the murder.

The murderous behaviour may easily be caused by socio-economic problems that have nothing to do with mental illness (Jones, 2000).

The essence of this chapter is that a perfectly 'normal' and law-abiding person can become a criminal (sometimes a violent criminal) if their circumstances are the right type for criminal activity. As Brookman (2005) wrote, murder is at the extreme ends of the spectrum but it is still nothing more than a crime.

Chapter II

Sociology and the criminal mind

In this chapter the relationship between society and murder will be dealt with, and why the incidence of murder is different across societies and changes with time in any given society. The relationship is not one-way: society affects the murder rate by making certain decisions rather than others and by having a specific culture, and murderers affect how society views murderers and crime in general – a relationship which can be heavily influenced by the media.

2.1 Why are there more killers in some societies than others?

Murder rates are not uniform across the world: they vary a lot between nations and also between different regions of any given nation. This in itself is an important piece of data because if different societies have different murder rates this must mean that the difference in the murder rate must be explained at least in part by differences of those societies.

In the first chapter, three important sociological theories of crime were discussed: all three theories essentially imply that being disadvantaged and poor makes crime, including murder, more likely. In this chapter it will be argued that two major mechanisms can account for differences in murder rates between societies: the level of disadvantage and socio-economic inequality experienced by the society, and cultural factors that are specific to the area. In essence, disadvantaged societies and those that have a high level of socio-economic inequality within them tend to have higher murder rates, and societies that have a more violent culture will also tend to have higher murder rates.

Many studies have found a very strong correlation between socio-economic inequality and crime rates. For example, Fajnzylber et al. (2002) studied crime rate and socio-economic data between 1970 and 1994 from 45 countries. They found that low economic growth and income inequality have a very strong predictive power for crime rates.

Another study that provides evidence for this relationship was done by Lederman et al. (2002), who studied national data from 39 countries from the period between 1980 and 1994. Like the previous study they found that income inequality and low economic growth have very strong and independent effects on violent crime. In other words, one of these effects by itself is sufficient to increase the incidence of violent crime, even if the other is absent.

These studies are consistent with the anomie theory of crime because it is quite obvious that socio-economic inequality will make anomie worse. Of course this would be even more convincing if it could be shown that socio-economic inequality has even stronger effects on homicide rates in countries that are overall quite wealthy. That is exactly what was found by Krahn et al. (1986): they found that not only does inequality increase homicide rates, but it does so much more strongly in wealthy countries. This might explain why homicide rates are so high in the United States, a country that is incredibly wealthy and yet at the same time as many poor, excluded and disadvantaged people: the perfect conditions for strong anomie to appear in many social groups. The effect of economic disadvantage on murder rate however is not exclusive to the United States: Nieuwbeerta et al. (2008) found that in the Netherlands economic disadvantage has a strong effect on the rate of homicide.

The other major sociological factor that may explain why different societies have different murder rates is culture. As mentioned in the last chapter, Wolfgang & Ferracuti (1981: 159) suggested that certain subcultures accept and encourage violence more than others, which can explain why their homicide rates are higher.

A very convincing correlation between culture and the incidence of male serial killers was found by DeFronzo et al. (2007). They assigned male serial killers to different states in the USA on the basis of where they spent their childhood and where they killed more victims. They found that western states such as California have a much higher incidence of serial killing than for example New England. These findings become meaningful when we look at the facts that the western and southern states have an old tradition of violence that in some cases goes back to when the states were founded. Of course in many southern states in the USA the death penalty is still used and in the southern states there is a much stronger use of 'honour violence' than in the rest of the USA (Burr & McCall 2003). On the other hand states like New England have traditionally been much more peaceful and have never used the death penalty. All of this very strongly suggests that some societies have higher murder rates than others simply because violence generally plays a bigger role in their culture, including the culture of the government itself.

There is another important factor that can make a big difference to the murder rate in a given society: population growth. Krahn et al. (1986) found that as population growth increases so does the murder rate. This is probably because societies with a higher population growth have more young people within them, and people between the ages of 15 and 25 are more likely to commit crimes, including murder, than any other age group (Levitt 2004).

2.2 Why do murder rates change over time?

Murder rates differ among societies but they also change with time within any given society. For example, the rate of homicide in the United States dropped by an incredible 43% between 1991 and 2001 – this was totally the opposite of what some of the greatest experts predicted (Levitt, 2004). Figure 1 shows the homicide rate in the United States between 1950 and 2001.

People mention many reasons for this sharp decline of the 1990's but Levitt found that four factors played a genuine role in the decline of homicide rate: increased rate of imprisonment, a reduction of the crack cocaine epidemic, the legalisation of abortion 20 years earlier, and increased police presence.

The reason for which imprisonment works in reducing homicide is simply that keeping criminals locked up prevents them from killing people outside. This is known as the *incapacitation* effect of prisons. It has an effect even when the criminal being locked up is not a convicted murderer, because people with prior convictions are more likely to commit murder than those who have never been convicted before (Dobash et al. 2004).

Figure 1: How homicide rate changed between 1950 and 2001 in the U.S.A. (*from Levitt 2004*).

Of course increasing the rate of imprisonment and the number of imprisonable offences also acts as a powerful deterrent.

The effect of imposing stricter sentences and increasing the prison population on crime rate was also independently shown by a study that focused on Texas (Spelman, cited in Muhlhausen 2007). In this particular study it was shown that increasing the prison population made a bigger contribution to crime reduction than any other factor.

The crack epidemic which began in 1985 was a major source of homicide in the United States, mainly as a result of violent rivalry between gangs. However the epidemic started to go down in the 1990's and this is another factor that contributed to the reduction of the homicide rate in the United States.

In 1973 the Supreme Court of the United States legalised abortion. This had a significant effect on the reduction of the homicide rate in the 1990 for three reasons: abortion reduces the rate of population growth and the number of young people between the ages of 15 and 25 that will be in the population years later, and as mentioned above this age bracket is the one that is most likely to commit violent crime. The other two reasons are that unwanted children are more likely to end up committing crimes, and parents with unwanted children are also more likely to commit crimes. This explains why the legalisation of abortion in the United States caused a major reduction in crime rates 20 years later.

Lastly, increasing police presence reduces crime, including homicide, by deterring impulse killings in public and also by ensuring that more criminals are caught and locked up – some of the petty criminals that are caught and imprisoned would have gone on to commit murders if they had not been caught.

Another reason for which the murder rate can change in a society is simply that a factor that normally favours it, such as social inequality, unemployment, poverty and lack of economic growth, is reduced. So for example if the social inequality described in the previous section is reduced by giving more opportunities to disadvantaged people it may be reasonable to expect that the murder rate will also go down.

2.3 Why do societies occasionally become obsessed with particular crimes at particular times?

It is very noticeable how society occasionally becomes very concerned by a particular type of crime although of course this happens more often with violent and shocking crimes. For example in May 2007 the UK became obsessed with child kidnappings after news was released of Madeleine McCann's kidnapping in Portugal. This researcher believes the answer to this question is quite straightforward: society learned of such incidents from the media and the reason for which society occasionally panics over one particular form of crime is that the media presented it in such a way as to cause that obsession. Similar obsession was produced by the murder of Holly Wells and Jessica Chapman by Ian Huntley in August 2002. Exactly the same thing happened in 1993 when James Bulger was killed in Liverpool by Jon Venables and Robert Thompson (two young children).

There are two chief mechanisms by which the media can control the preoccupation of society with particular crimes: by over-emphasising particular incidents and creating panic (as with the three cases mentioned above) and by being very selective with what type of crimes (and what types of murder) they report. The media has a strong tendency to exaggerate and inflate murder reports (Jenkins 1994: 97). 'Tabloid' newspapers are particularly fond of presenting murders and other crimes in an exaggerated and simplistic way. Peelo et *al.* (2004) found that newspapers are much more likely to report murders if they involve sex, financial gain, jealousy or revenge. On the other hand killings that happen in bar fights are much less likely to be reported. I do not think this is a coincidence: people who commit murder in bar fights are almost never labeled as monsters, whereas people who commit serial killings or kill for sexual reasons tend to be labeled as monsters that are completely different to us. As they put it, the media play a very big role in establishing the 'othernesses of murderers (Peelo et *al.* 2004: 256). This makes a very big contribution to society's perception of murder as a crime that is in a different class to all other crimes – a view which this dissertation strongly disagrees with. The media's behaviour and presentation of murders in this researcher's opinion answers the question posed by D'Cruze et *al.* (2006: 21): why do most people perceive murderers as 'not us'?

The entertainment industry also makes a contribution to society's perception of murderers as 'not us' because it loves to present serial killers as monsters (Jenkins 1994: 96).

In this chapter the relationship between murder and society was examined. Society can affect the murder rate through its culture (which may encourage violence to varying extents), economic growth, social inequality, population growth and other socio-economic parameters. Society may also affect the murder rate with mechanisms such as imprisonment, tough sentencing and heavily investing on police. All of this means that different murder rates will be found in different societies, and murder rates can also change within a society. Lastly, it was considered how society can become obsessed and panicked by particular forms of crime, including murder, if the media is selective in which murders it reports and exaggerates their seriousness.

Chapter III

Murder and masculinity

The statistics are very clear: murder is a very male crime (D'Cruze et *al.* 2006: 21). This chapter will deal with the issue of murder and masculinity and its relevance to male serial killers. It will be seen that masculinity plays a very big role in how male murderers perceive themselves, and often results in murder in situations that normally would not be thought of as being particularly violent. In other situations masculine desire for possession and control probably plays a very big role, particularly with serial killers.

The greatest predictor of murderous behaviour is the male gender and the Y chromosome. 89% of identified murderers in England and Wales are men (Levi & Maguire 2002). In domestic violence, 86% of cases involve males attacked by men whereas 8% of cases involve men attacked by women (Heidensohn, 2002). It therefore appears that women are more likely to be killed by men than men are to be killed by women, and that men kill a lot more than women in general. This raises the important question of why. There is fairly wide agreement that probably the major reason for this is the different roles given to men and women by society. Of course men have traditionally occupied dominant roles in society and this will be discussed later as one of the possible reasons behind male violence, but an important point worth making is that males and females are treated differently from the beginning of their lives: from the very beginning boys tend to be given more freedom whereas girls are given greater protection and more constraints – and this is one possible reason for which women tend to be more law-abiding than men. This is supported by the fact that when social constraints and gender roles are removed, as might be the case with broken families, women commit just as much crime as men (Rock 2002: 58).

A central topic in murder and masculinity is male dominance and its relevance to the act of killing. As mentioned above, males have traditionally occupied dominant roles in society and their greater tendency to murder may be seen as an inevitable consequence of their hegemony. This idea gained popularity when Cameron and Frazer published their analysis of the Yorkshire Ripper, Peter Sutcliffe (D'Cruze et *al.* 2006: 38) – they argued that the Yorkshire Ripper's activities were an extension and magnification of the male act of penetration. In this case the male exerted ultimate dominance over many females by killing them.

The examination of serial killers such as Harold Shipman and Dennis Nilsen reveals a potentially important role of the male perception of control in murder. For example, Harold Shipman, who was a successful doctor in Hyde (Greater Manchester), killed large numbers of patients, mostly elderly female victims, by giving them lethal injections of diamorphine. The case is a particularly interesting one because Shipman did not fall into the category of people that are most likely to commit murders: he was a doctor and therefore highly educated, well paid and highly respected in his community. Psychological analysis after his arrest revealed that Shipman was terrified by the idea of not being in control, and therefore his killings may be explained in terms of his attempt to force his control over circumstances that were not always within his control ((D'Cruze et *al.* 2006: 33). In other words, Shipman killed elderly patients because that was the only way to have true and complete control over their fates. If he had let them live he would not have been able to guarantee one outcome or the other (life or death), which of course applies to all doctors. So even though Harold Shipman's murders were not of a sexual nature, masculinity still played a role because it was Shipman's need for control (a very masculine characteristic) that drove him to murder, if the analysis made by the psychologists is meaningful.

An even more extreme example of how the masculine need for control led to murderous behaviour is that of British homosexual sexual serial killer Dennis Nilsen. He was extremely frustrated by the fact that he was unable to maintain a relationship with another man for more than a few days, and the solution he found to his problem was to kill the young men he brought back to his flat. He kept the bodies in his flat for weeks or months, bathing them, watching television with them and talking to them (D'Cruze et *al.* 2006: 143). By his own admission this was the only way in which Nilsen could enjoy long-lasting relationships and complete control over young men.

The concept of control extends to hatred, which was the primary motivation of serial killer Edmund Kemper – he stated clearly that whenever he murdered a young girl in his mind it was his mother he was trying to murder (Holmes *et al.* 1998: 54). This fits in with the idea that some (definitely not all) femicides committed by men are caused by misogyny, which is the hatred of women. Feminist authors are convinced that misogyny plays a very important role for the male serial killers (Jenkins 1994: 142).

According to Polk (1994) men resort to murder in a variety of situations: in sexual contacts, in violent confrontations, during the course of other crimes, and as a means by which they can resolve conflicts. The unifying idea here is that in each of these situations the possibility arises for a man's masculinity to be challenged, which can drive the man in question to murder. Many of these murders are often caused by very minor incidents, but the male preoccupation with the defence of his masculine image and honour ensures that they escalate to murder (Polk 1994: 61). The big role played by masculine pride is shown by the fact that men are more likely to murder if their masculinity is challenged in front of other men rather than in front of a female audience (Polk 1994: 78). Hence it would appear that many murders committed by men are absolutely not planned or foreseen in any way, which lends some support to this dissertation's argument; because it shows that most murderers are not monsters at all, but fairly normal men who took things too far. This concept is echoed by D'Cruze et al. (2006: 105), who suggest that intimate murders are nothing more than the 'miscalibration of domestic violence.'

It is also worth enquiring into how murderers perceive their own masculinity. It seems clear that Nilsen was made to feel extremely inadequate by the fact that no partner was ever willing to stay with him for more than a few days, and he himself stated that he was very lonely (D'Cruze et al. 2006: 143). Similarly it has been suggested that Ted Bundy was driven to kill many young ladies by the hatred he felt for a girlfriend who rejected him, although this idea has been challenged and does not seem consistent with Ted Bundy's character (Holmes et al. 1998: 53). In fact, in many ways Ted Bundy does not fit the profile of a sexually frustrated and dissatisfied male: he was considerably attractive and very skilled at persuading young women to get into his car, for example.

There is another way in which masculinity is of great importance to the subject of murder: traditional gender roles in society mean that men are expected to be the breadwinner, be more ambitious, make more money and have more authority than women. This researcher believes that this makes men strongly susceptible to the effects of anomie and strain, since these theories state that crime in general and murder in particular are more likely to be committed by people who are extremely frustrated with their inability to make their financial and social dreams come true. This researcher would also argue that masculinity also makes men more susceptible to differential association, partly because the strong societal pressure they feel to make money can make differential association have a stronger effect (anomie will make them dissatisfied, which in turn will encourage them to spend more time with men who have achieved financial and social success through criminal activity, without the hurdles imposed by the law). This would explain why most murders committed by men involve strangers or acquaintances rather than intimates: it is because murders motivated by financial, professional or social status frustrations are much more likely to involve strangers, rivals and business partners rather than family members or spouses. It would also explain why women, who feel much less pressure to become wealthy and be the breadwinner and financially independent, exhibit the opposite pattern and mostly kill family members and sexual partners in the domestic context. This researcher believes that different roles assigned to men and women by society account at least in part for the different patterns shown by male and female murderers. Some researchers, such as Jensen (2001: 2) tend to agree with this.

Conclusion

This chapter has examined the crucial topic of masculinity and how it relates to male murderers, who are responsible for the vast majority of murders committed in society. It may be stated that men are more likely to commit murder than women because society has always allocated the aggressive and dominant role to men. This may result in murder when the man in question sees no other way to assert or maintain his control. In some extreme cases, such as those of Peter Sutcliffe, Harold Shipman and Dennis Nilsen, an obsessive desire for control that cannot be satisfied by normal life led to the murder of several people. In the case of Dennis Nilsen we can be very confident of this interpretation because he openly admitted to it in the detailed confessions he gave to the police. The chapter also examined how the male concept of masculinity can occasionally cause very normal men to murder if they feel that their masculinity has been challenged, particularly if it happened in front of other men.

Chapter IV

Women and murder

In the previous chapter the point was made that murder is a very male crime. However, women also murder, sometimes with considerable cruelty and apparent lack of motive, so this chapter will explore the relationship between femininity and murder. Femininity is relevant to murders perpetrated by women in two main respects: murders perpetrated by women exhibit a very different pattern to those perpetrated by men, and the issue of gender and femininity can also make a difference to how female murderers are treated by the judicial system and how they are perceived by society. The issue of whether women kill for radically different reasons to men will also be considered, with particular reference to female serial killers.

In addition to the issue of quantity, homicide perpetrated by men and women also differs a lot in terms of the pattern of the victims. Specifically, a greater proportion of murders committed by women involved victims that the murderer knew intimately: spouse, sexual partners and family members are the most common victims of female murderers (Kellerman, 1992), whereas the most common victims of male murderers are strangers or acquaintances. Also women mostly kill in a household (Jensen 2001: 2). This pattern has been used to argue that women mostly use murder as the only way to escape abusive relationships and dangerous situations at home, and indeed one study found that the fewer options are available to women who experienced domestic violence; the more likely they are to commit murder (Browne & Williams 1989). This is hardly surprising. There can be no doubt that women suffer domestic violence at the hands of men more than men suffer domestic violence at the hands of women, and therefore that murders committed by women tend to involve domestic and relationship issues. That said, there is a strong possibility that men may underreport incidents in which they experienced physical abuse from women (Heidensohn, 2002). Hence domestic violence and partner abuse is undoubtedly one of the major motives behind women who murder More generally it has been argued that gender roles in society are the principal reason which female murderers exist at all (Jensen 2001: 2). It will be explained later in this chapter that gender inequality cannot possibly account for all female murderers.

Another implication of the fact that women are generally more likely to kill intimates rather than strangers is that it raises the question of whether traditional criminological theories are applicable to them. For example, strain theory suggests that people are more likely to commit murder if they are disadvantaged and there is a big gap between their expectations and what society actually gives them. The point here is that these murders are likely to be motivated by financial gain, anger or frustration, but women do not kill intimates for these reasons: when women kill a family member or a spouse it tends to be to escape violence, or for jealousy. It has nothing to do with economic dissatisfaction. This is known as the problem of 'generalisability' of criminological theories (Jensen 2001: 16; Heidensohn 2002: 517).

Femininity is an important concept here and in fact it is the only reason for which society still finds it very shocking when women commit violent crimes. The idea of femininity is familiar to everyone: females in most if not all societies are thought of as being submissive, physically weaker, compliant, less determined, with inferior leadership abilities, nurturing, motherly and so on (Jenkins 1994: 152). This is probably the reason for which certain feminist authors feel the need to provide special explanations for female murderers, when in fact it has been observed that women commit just as many violent offences as men when gender constraints are removed (Rock 2002:58) and of course the many female serial killers in history show that 'evil' is not gender-specific.

Society's expectations regarding femininity can work both for and against female murderers. There is some evidence that chivalry – the other side of the coin of femininity – can mean that women are likely to be given more lenient sentences than men, other things being equal (Heidensohn 2002: 503). There is a lot of anecdotal evidence for this. That said, society's concept of femininity can also work heavily against female murderers: when a female murderer is not perceived by society as conforming to its ideal of femininity, she tends to be judged a lot more harshly than the average murderer, and she's also more likely to receive slightly harsher treatment from the authorities.

Examples of female murderers who defied society's notion of femininity and propriety and therefore received harsher treatment than would normally be expected are the British domestic servant Kate Webster (D'Cruze et al. 2006: 52), the serial killer of babies Beverly Allitt and Ruth Ellis, who shot her lover in the back. In fact there are two distinct ways in which women can fail to match society's expectations of women: either by not being feminine (in other words by being masculine, dominant and not sexually alluring) or by being excessively attractive and confident, which immediately makes people think she is sexually liberated and promiscuous. One of these conditions is sufficient to place a female murderer at a disadvantage. Ruth Ellis, for example, would have been much better off appearing in court as a frail female victim, rather than an attractive, confident and extremely sexual lady.

More recently it was found that women are significantly more likely to be arrested on suspicion of murder if they deviate from society's perception of female propriety: in other words females are more likely to be arrested on suspicion of murder if they are not a homemaker, a devoted mother or loyal wife (Visher, 1983). Of course if the female in question is a prostitute or sexually promiscuous, she will be treated very unsympathetically by the police, in the court room and by society in general. The fact that Aileen Wuornos was a prostitute undoubtedly did not help her during the trial and after her sentence. Interestingly, femininity is also relevant to female victims and to the fate of their murderer: for example when the body of Carol Park was recovered from a lake she was wearing a sexually alluring blue nylon 'nightie'. This made her look sexually liberated and potentially promiscuous, which made the police investigation less enthusiastic and delayed the conviction of her murderer, her husband Gordon Park, by many years (D'Cruze et al. 2006: 110).

The question of female serial killers will now be dealt with. A serial killer is generally defined as a person who kills three or more people over a time span of at least several weeks, usually months or years. There is a cooling off period in between murders (Holmes et al. 1998: 45). Sex is not involved in the definition of serial killers, so even if it is true that females rarely if ever kill to satisfy sexual fantasies, this does not mean that females cannot be serial killers. The concept of female serial killers has been considered politically incorrect and unacceptable by feminist researchers (Jenkins 1994: 151). However, their assertion that there is no such thing as female serial killers is simply incorrect: between 10 and 15% of American serial killers have been female (Jenkins

1994: 151), including Aileen Wuornos, who killed seven men, and Amy Archer Gilligan, who was arguably 'the most prolific serial killer in American history' (Jenkins 1994: 151). Another incredibly strong example of a female serial killer is that of Beverly Allitt, a British nurse who murdered four children by injecting them with potassium or insulin (D'Cruze et *al.* 2006: 61). The case of Beverly Allitt is perhaps the most shocking one for society, because women are understandably thought of as being very maternal and caring with children, but this particular woman killed children not by being negligent, but by deliberately injecting them with substances that caused cardiac arrests.

The existence of female serial killers is very important to this chapter and to the entire dissertation, because female serial killers kill for very different reasons to the women who kill their husbands, lovers or family members. In other words, female serial killers are very similar to male murderers in general because they kill strangers rather than intimates. It also contributes to this dissertation's general argument that virtually anyone is capable of murder under certain circumstances and that murder is therefore nothing more than a very damaging crime. Furthermore, it very strongly shows that gender inequality by itself cannot completely explain the phenomenology of female murders.

Conclusion

In this chapter it was seen that female murderers differ from male murderers both in their activity (women commit fewer murders than men) and also in the pattern: female murderers mostly kill partners, family members and other intimate acquaintances, whereas men kill mostly random acquaintances and strangers. The statement that female murderers are therefore largely motivated by abuse and a feeling of helplessness undoubtedly has some merit. It was also discussed that contrary to what some researchers state, there have been plenty of vicious female serial killers in society, and they are of interest to this dissertation because they are quite similar to men, in the sense that they tend to kill strangers and people they are not close to. The issue of femininity and how it affects the treatment of female murderers and their perception by society was also discussed. Society's expectations of femininity usually mean that women who kill are viewed with particular shock by society. The specific female murderer's femininity also plays a role: women who conform to society's expectations of females are less likely to be arrested and receive more lenient sentences if they are convicted of murder, other things being equal.

Chapter V

Victims

Exclusive focus has been given so far to murderers. This work will now turn to the victims. There are two types of victims: the person killed by the murderer, and the family members or close friends of the person who was killed. This chapter will deal mainly with the consequences suffered by homicide survivors; as we will see, the harm perpetrated by killers is not limited to ending a person's life violently and prematurely: a great deal of suffering, which sometimes lasts a lifetime, is also inflicted to those who were very close to the victim, and to those who were somehow directly involved in the murder. In this chapter the term 'homicide survivors' shall be used interchangeably to refer to people who were very close to the primary victim or someone who narrowly escaped being murdered.

The direct victim of homicide rarely if ever receives the same amount of attention as the murderer who committed the crime – for this reason the murder victim is in many ways the 'forgotten actor' (Zedner 2002: 719). When the victim does receive attention it is almost always in the context of reducing the murderer's culpability by highlighting aspects of the victim's life that in some way failed to match society's expectations. As was discussed in the preceding chapters, the female victims who are in some way suspected to have been very sexual, masculine or 'unconventional' in some other way can make the police less careful with its investigation and can make society as a whole feel much less sorry for the victim. This was the case of Carol Park, who was murdered by her husband Gordon Park. In this particular case the mere fact that the victim was wearing a provocative 'nightie' when her body was found almost allowed the murderer to get away with it.

This is closely related to the concept of victim-precipitated crime. It is undoubtedly true that in some cases the victim specifically did something that made the murder more likely – for example, one study found that 26% of murders committed in Philadelphia between 1948 and 1952 were victim-precipitated (Wolfgang, 1958, cited in Zedner 2002: 420). However in many cases society perceives that the murder was caused by the victim for futile and superficial reasons – an obvious example is when the female body is found wearing provocative clothing and society immediately claims that 'she asked for it.'

Even if the murderer is caught and successfully convicted and locked away from society, the effects of his or her actions continue to cause great pain to homicide survivors for many years to come. There are two distinguishable ways in which homicide survivors suffer considerable pain in the aftermath of the murder: intense grief and post-traumatic stress on the one hand, and the treatment they receive from society and the judicial system on the other. In both cases homicide survivors get a very bad deal.

The way in which homicide survivors are treated by the court system can be intensely traumatic and frustrating. For example, homicide survivors are almost universally dissatisfied with the fact that murder is treated in court as a crime against the State, not against the primary and secondary victims (Zedner 2002: 444). They are also greatly distressed by the fact that the murder victim is rarely referred to by name in court, but always with terms such as 'the deceased,' 'the corpse' and so on (Magee, 1983). Furthermore in the United Kingdom victims are not given the chance to express their views on the appropriate sentence to be imposed, whereas in the United States they are allowed to make a statement in court and to express their views on the matter (Zedner, 2002).

The legal system can also be exceptionally insensitive to the feelings of homicide survivors. Bob Hart, whose wife and son were brutally murdered by a neighbour in Connecticut, was heartbroken to discover that the defendant, Larry Gates, was negotiating a plea bargain with the prosecutor. The deal was that Larry Gates would admit two counts of first-degree murder in return for the dropping of all other charges against him. Although the plea bargain resulted in Larry Gates receiving a hefty custodial sentence, Bob Hart was upset by the fact that obtaining justice for the brutal murder of his wife and son eventually boiled down to bargaining deals behind his back (Zedner 2002: 21).

The suffering and stigmatisation that homicide survivors have to endure can get even worse: when Betty Jane Spencer was lined up and shot with her four sons in her home in Indiana (USA) by four armed robbers, her four sons were killed but she miraculously survived. It was not only the loss of her four sons that she had to endure in the aftermath of the murder – a rumour soon developed in her town that the whole incident was planned by her and her husband in order to profit from the life insurance of the boys (Zedner 2002: 59). Fortunately she was able to recognize one of the men from mugshots in police records and she successfully testified in court and the men were convicted. This particular case also illustrates the role that homicide survivors can play in the identification and successful prosecution of murderers: it is extremely unlikely that the murderers would have been caught in this case if Betty Jane Spencer had not meticulously examined hundreds of 'mugshots' at the police station.

Another way in which victims feel abused by the judicial system is the fact that they are not allowed to attend the trial as members of the public if they are also witnesses (Asaro, 1995).

Intense media attention can make the pain of homicide survivors even worse: loss of privacy is one of the major consequences faced by secondary victims particularly if the murder is a very high profile one (Asaro, 1995). Betty Jane Spencer, for example, even after being regarded as a local hero after playing a decisive role in the prosecution and conviction of the murderers, felt seriously depressed and socially isolated (Magee 1983: 65), and the murders strained the relationship between Betty Jane and her family. She also had persistent psychological problems and started seeing a psychiatrist (Magee 1983: 69).

It is indeed quite common for homicide survivors to experience serious and long lasting problems of mental health in the aftermath of the murder. These psychological difficulties typically have two phases: in the first phase the secondary victims experience feelings of denial, impaired eating patterns, and a strong feeling of confusion; in the second phase, depression, a sense of helplessness, acute fear and a strong desire for revenge set in (Asaro, 1995). There is also a significantly increased risk of post-traumatic stress disorder, which has symptoms such as reliving the incident, deliberately avoiding places or people who are in some way associated with the murder and an exaggerated startle response (Asaro, 1995).

The consequences suffered by homicide survivors are illustrated by the girls who survived Ted Bundy's Omega Chi massacre at Florida State University (January 1978). In the year following Bundy's attack, two of the sorority members dropped out of their university course, and one committed suicide (Rubin, 1998). Another survivor, Susan Denton, experienced persistent nightmares on a nightly basis in the years following the Omega Chi sorority massacre (Rubin, 1998).

All in all there is a huge body of evidence that shows that murder takes a very heavy toll on homicide survivors, even though society has a strong tendency to focus on the murderer and often forgets the victim. Homicide survivors are given even less attention, unless the media thinks they make a good story, in which case they are harassed. One study showed that 75% of victims of violence are still affected by the incident between two and five years later (Shapland et *al.* 1985, cited in Zedner 2002). For this reason many victim support groups have been started all over the world.

Conclusion

(So how do societies perceive murder?)

This project has examined a wide variety of issues concerning murder and murderers. The major sociological theories of crime were discussed with reference to the Chicago School, anomie theory and its subcategory, Sutherland's Differential Association. It was discussed in this chapter that a number of sociological conditions, particularly highly zoned urban environments and a substantial gap between individuals' expectations and what society actually allowed them to achieve, can lead to higher rates of crime, including murder. This in itself supports my argument that murder is an ordinary crime, because if murder was only something committed by people who are genuinely 'not like us', then surely sociological factors would not make such a big difference to the murder rate.

In the second chapter it was seen that murder rates vary between societies and also change with time in any given society. There is very strong evidence that certain factors make a very big difference to the murder rate: population growth has an effect on the murder rate because societies with a high population growth have more young people, and young people are those that are more likely to perpetrate violent crimes. The crack cocaine epidemic which started in 1985 had a large effect on murder rates, mostly by causing violent competition between young gangs. When the crack cocaine epidemic began to recede in the early 90s, this was immediately matched by a reduction in the murder rate. Another factor that can have a big effect on murder rate is the rate of imprisonment: several studies have now convincingly showed that imposing stiffer sentences and increasing the prison population reduces the murder rate. All of this shows very clearly that murder is simply an extension of crime and that the rate at which it is committed can be reduced with crime-reducing measures just as with any other crime. Furthermore, culture can have a very big effect on murder rate, as shown by the study of DeFronzo et al. (2007) – yet another study that suggests that murderous behaviour can appear anywhere if the conditions are right.

The third chapter explored the relationship between murder and masculinity. A very popular belief among criminologists is that murder, particularly in the context of serial killers, is sometimes the result of the male desire to have a high level of control.

Masculine self-perception also plays a role and it was seen how seemingly innocent situations can result in murder if a man's masculinity is challenged, particularly if it happens in front of other men. Men are much more susceptible to anomie and Differential Association affects than women. The fact that the rate of murder committed by men can be modulated by social inequality and the specific company they keep once again shows that murder is not in a different class from other crimes, but is simply a particularly intense crime that often results from the miss-calibration of certain behaviours such as domestic violence. A particularly convincing study that supports this was done by Dobash et *al.* (2007), who found that the childhood problems of late-onset murderers are very similar to the childhood problems of non-murderers, whereas their adulthood difficulties are very similar to those of early-onset murderers (unemployment, social frustration, drug abuse and so on). In this researcher's opinion this is one more piece of evidence that shows that almost anyone can commit murder if the circumstances are right, even if they started off in the non-offending category.

The fourth chapter examined the phenomenon of women who murder and how this relates to the concept of femininity. It was discussed how society has of very well defined idea of what women should be like and this has two consequences: society is particularly shocked when females commit violent murders, and they are also more likely to be judged harshly as a result of their deviation from social expectations. The central idea here is that violent female murderers have taken society by surprise, since the idea of female murderers, particularly female serial killers, is accepted with great difficulty by society and is violently rejected by feminists. However, as many as 10% to 15% of serial killers have been female, including some particularly dangerous and elusive ones like Beverly Allitt and Aileen Wuornos. Additionally it has been shown that when gender-specific constraints and socialisation is removed, women offend just as much as men (Rock, 2002). Hence murder cannot really be seen as a categorically different crime that is only committed by male 'monsters'.

The last chapter focused on victims, particularly secondary victims or 'homicide survivors'. In addition to the obvious loss that homicide survivors suffer, the cold treatment of the judicial system and the obsessive, non-supportive attention of society makes things worse. This 'secondary victimization' (Zedner 2002: 419), together with the loss of a loved one in tragic circumstances, tends to have long-lasting social and psychological consequences on these victims.

This dissertation has attempted to argue that the crime of murder should not be placed in a category of its own. Some researchers, such as Wilson (2007), have also argued that regarding murder as an exceptional crime is an old-fashioned way of looking at things and produces unhelpful legislation such as mandatory sentences. The philosophy of mandatory sentences is that murder has a 'symbolic moral uniqueness' (Wilson 2007: 158). The central argument of this dissertation is that murder should *not* be seen as having a special status in any way. Taking this view would also make it easier to achieve greater justice by allowing varying degrees of culpability, as Wilson suggested (Wilson, 2007). This work's main argument was supported by showing that all genders, all social classes and all personality types can commit murder. This is reinforced by the fact that tweaking variables such as social inequality, economic growth and culture can have a very big effect on the murder rate. That the murder rate also depends on the cultural acceptance of violence by different societies, as shown by DeFronzo et *al.* (2007), is an even more convincing demonstration that murder is nothing more and nothing less than a crime.

The media love to report murders in an exaggerated way, and love to encourage the idea that murderers are 'monsters' and fundamentally different to 'normal' people, when in fact if we set aside the enormous pain that it causes survivors, murder is 'banal' (D'Cruze et al. 2006: 29). Society has a strong tendency to look at murderers as fundamentally evil, but it would greatly benefit by looking at murder more dispassionately and less as a manifestation of monstrosity.

References

Adler, F. and Laufer, W. S. (1995) *The Legacy of Anomie Theory*. New Jersey: Transaction Publishers.

Asaro, M. R. (1995) 'Reactions of Surviving Family Members', pp. 120-123 in Gerdes, L. (eds.) Serial Killers. San Diego: Greenhaven Press.

Bernard, T. J. (1984) 'Control Criticisms of Strain Theories: An Assessment of Theoretical and Empirical Adequacy', *Journal of Research in crime and delinquency*, 21(4)
pp 353.372.

Brookman, F. (2005) *Understanding Homicide*. London: Sage.

Browne, A. and Williams, K. R. (1989) 'Exploring the Effect of Resource Availability and The Likelihood of Female-Perpetrated Homicide', *Law and Society Review*, 23(1) pp 75.94.

Burr, A. and McCall, P. L. (2003) 'The Enduring Puzzle of Southern Homicide: Is Regional Religious Culture the Missing Piece?', *Homicide Studies*, 7(4) pp 326.352.

D'Cruze, S. Walklate, S. Pegg, S. (2006) Murder: Social and Historical Approaches to Understanding Murder and Murderers. Devon: Willan Publishing.

DeFronzo, J., Ditta, A., Hannon, L. Prochnow, J. (2007) 'Male Serial Homicide: The Influence of Cultural and Structural Variables', *Homicide Studies*, 11(1) pp 3.14.

Dobash, R. E., Dobash, R. P., Cavanagh, K. Lewis, R. (2004) Not an ordinary killer - Just an ordinary guy, *Violence Against Women*, 10(6) pp 577.605.

Dobash, R. P. Dobash, R. E. Cavanagh, K. Medina-Ariza, J. (2007) 'Onset of Offending and Life Course Among Men Convicted of Murder', *Homicide Studies*, 11(4) pp 243.271.

Fajnzylber, P. Lederman, D. Loayza, N. (2002) 'What Causes Violent Crime?', *European Economic Review*, 46 pp 1323.1357.

FBI (no date) 'Crime in the United States: Uniform Crime Reports', http://www.fbi.gov/ucr/ucr.htm, accessed 27/04/08.

Glueck, S. (1956) 'Theory and Fact in Criminology: A Criticism of Differential Association', *British Journal of Delinquency*, 7 pp. 92.109.

Heidensohn, F. (2002) 'Gender and Crime', pp. 491-530 in Maguire, M. Morgan, R. Reiner, R. (eds.) The Oxford Handbook of Criminology. Oxford: Oxford University Press.

Holmes, R. M., De Deburger, J. Holmes, S. T. (1998) *Serial Murder*. London: Sage Publications.

Jenkins, P. (1994) *Using Murder: The Social Construction of Serial Homicide*. New York: Aldine De Gruyter.

Jensen, V. (2001) *Why Women Kill: Homicide and Gender Equality*. Boulder: Lynne Rienner Publishers.

Jones, S. (2000) *Understanding Violent Crime*. Milton Keynes: Open University Books.

Kellermann, A. L. Mercy, J. A. (1992) 'Men, Women, and Murder: Gender-Specific Differences in Rates of Fatal Violence and Victimization', *J Trauma* 33(1) pp 1.5.

Kim, S-W and Pridemore, W. A. (2005) 'Poverty, Socioeconomic Change, Institutional Anomie, and Homicide', *Social Science Quarterly* 86(S1) pp 1377.1398.

Kornhauser, R. R. (1978) *Social Sources of Delinquency*. Chicago: University of Chicago Press.

Krahn, H. Hartnagel, T. F. Gartrell, J. W. (1986) 'Income Inequality and Homicide Rates: Cross-National Data and Criminological Theories', *Criminology*, 24(2) pp 269.294.

Lederman, D. Loayza, N. Menéndez, A. M. (2002) 'Violent Crime: Does Social Capital Matter?', *Economic Development and Cultural Change*, 50 pp 509.539.

Levi, M. and Maguire, M. (2002) 'Violent Crime', pp. 795-843 in Maguire, M. Morgan, R. & Reiner, R. (eds.) *The Oxford Handbook of Criminology*. Oxford: Oxford University Press.

Levitt, S D. (2004) 'Understanding Why Crime Fell in the 1990s: Four Factors That explain the Decline and Six That Do Not', *Journal of Economic Perspectives*, 18(1) pp 163.190.

Magee, D. (1983) *What Murder Leaves Behind*. New York: Dodd, Mead & Company.

Muhlhausen, D. B. (2007) 'Changing Crime Rates: Ineffective Law Enforcement Grants and The Prison Buildup', *the Heritage Foundation*, 12 February, http://www.heritage.org/Research/Crime/wm1355.cfm, accessed 28/04/08.

Nieuwbeerta, P. McCall, P. L. Elffers, H. Wittebrood, K. (2008) 'Neighborhood Characteristics and Individual Homicide Risks: Effects of Social Cohesion, Confidence in the Police, and Socioeconomic Disadvantage', *Homicide Studies*, 12(1) pp 90.116.

Peelo, M., Francis, B., Soothill, K., Pearson, J. Ackerley, E. (2004) *British Journal of Criminology* 44 pp 256.275.

Polk, K. (1994) *When Men Kill: Scenarios of Masculine Violence*. Cambridge: Cambridge University Press.

Rubin, S. (1998) 'Lives Forever Changed: Surviving Serial Killer Ted Bundy', pp. 124-131 in Gerdes, L. (eds.) Serial Killers. San Diego: Greenhaven Press

Rock, P. (2002) 'Sociological Theories of Crime', pp. 51-82 in Maguire, M. Morgan, R. & Reiner, R. (eds.) The Oxford Handbook of Criminology. Oxford: Oxford University Press.

Sutherland, E. H. (1947 4th edn.) *Principles of Criminology*. Philadelphia: J.B. Lippincott.

Visher, C. A. (1983) 'Gender, Police Arrest Decisions, and Notions of Chivalry', *Criminology*, 21(1) pp. 5.28.

Vold, G. B. Bernard, T. J. Snipes, J. B. (2002 5th ed.) *Theoretical Criminology*. Oxford: Oxford University Press.

Wilson, W. (2007) 'What's wrong with murder?', *Crime, Law and Philosophy*, 1 pp 157.177.

Wolfgang, M. E. and Ferracuti, F. (1981) *The Subculture of Violence*. California: Sage Publications.

Zedner, L. (2002) 'Victims', pp. 419-456 in Maguire, M. Morgan, R. Reiner, R. (eds.) The Oxford Handbook of Criminology. Oxford: Oxford University Press.

www.ingramcontent.com/pod-product-compliance
Lightning Source LLC
Chambersburg PA
CBHW070236290526
45789CB00004B/1644